TEACHING ENGLISH IN THE NATIONAL CURRICULUM

MEDIA EDUCATION

Cary Bazalgette

Series Editor: Patrick Scott

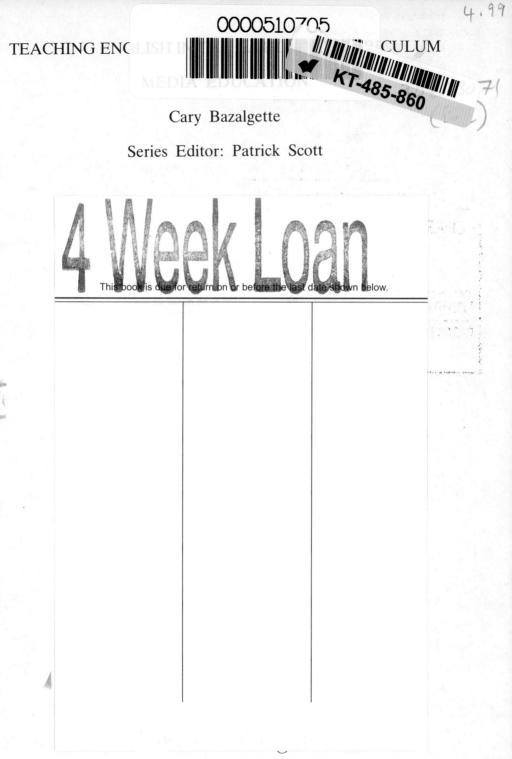

4 Week Loan

This book is due for return on or before the last date shown below.

LONDON SYDNEY AUCKLAND TORONTO

ACKNOWLEDGMENTS

The author and publishers would like to thank the following for permission to reproduce illustrations:

The National Portrait Gallery, London (p.11, top); The Guardian (p.11, bottom and p.32); British Broadcasting Council (p.22, left); GQ, Condé Nast Publications (p.22 right); CIC Video (p.23); Viz (p.24); Philip Sydney (p.34, top); Tom Mustoe and Simon Howarth (p.34, bottom); The English and Media Centre, London (pp.35 and 36); Ann Lines, Chesworth County Junior School, Horsham (p.54).

British Library Cataloguing in Publication Data
Bazalgette, Cary
  Media education. – (Teaching English in the
  National Curriculum)
  I. Title II. Series
  302.23071

  ISBN 0–340–53695–0

First published 1991

© 1991 Cary Bazalgette

Produced by Serif Tree, Kidlington, Oxon.
Printed in Great Britain for the educational publishing division of Hodder & Stoughton Ltd, Mill Road, Dunton Green, Sevenoaks, Kent by St Edmundsbury Press Ltd.

CONTENTS

Chapter 1
You and the Media   2

Chapter 2
'Reading' Texts   8

Chapter 3
'Reading' Texts in the Classroom   19

Chapter 4
Making Texts: Discovering the Language   27

Chapter 5
Making Texts: For Whom and Why?   39

Chapter 6
Progress and Planning   50

Resources   60

You and the Media

> We need a common culture, not for the sake of an abstraction,
> but because we shall not survive without it.
>   (Raymond Williams, *Culture and Society*)

You are looking at the first page of a book. It may be the first
time you have looked at it, in which case you may be deciding
whether to read it. Many factors will influence that decision, and
what I write here and now will only be one of them. 'Here', for
me, is a computer screen in a house in North London; 'now' is
a sunny Saturday morning in April 1990. I don't know who you
are, or where you are now. The processes that will intervene
between what I write and what you read are mostly out of my
control. Editors, copy editors, designers, printers, marketing
managers and distributors will all put in their own efforts to try
to make you read on, buy the book and recommend it to others.
Reviewers, education advisers, your own friends and colleagues
may have done the same; or they may have done the opposite.
Your own professional experiences and your skills as a reader
will enable you to categorise this book, to make predictions
about what the rest of it will be like, and to decide whether or
not it will be useful, interesting or pleasurable to you in your
own 'here and now'.

   Similar processes stand between you and the producers of
most of the things you watch on film, television or video, or
listen to on the radio, as well as what you read. Indeed, the
number of 'texts' you read/watch/listen to that reach you directly
from an individual producer is probably quite limited: letters,
photographs, maybe answerphone messages, and, if you are a
teacher, writing and artwork produced by your pupils. Likewise,
the number of texts through which you as a writer (or a
photographer, or video maker, or whatever) reach other people
directly is also probably quite limited. And even these 'private'
texts are likely to conform to generally agreed conventions: the
way letters or essays are set out; the way people are supposed
to get in a group and smile at the camera.

   My aim in this book is to argue that it is worth knowing more
about the processes through which texts – both 'public' and
'private' – reach people. If it is worth knowing about these

processes, it follows therefore that children can enjoy learning about them, and I shall describe ways of enabling them to do this. My arguments are not based on a notion that such processes are sinister or manipulative, and obscure or subvert 'true meaning' (although sometimes of course they can); but on the belief that such processes are *part* of the meaning of any text. Nor am I using the word 'processes' to mean just the technical or commercial methods through which texts are produced: people's choices, preferences, tastes and experiences are also parts of these processes. Learning more about them gives us more power over the texts we read and the texts we produce. The ideas I shall use in this book and the teaching approaches I shall describe are part of what is getting to be generally known as 'media education', but they are not necessarily the same as other accounts of media education that you may have read or heard.

To me, it makes no sense to propose 'the media' as a separate bit of the curriculum, or indeed as something that has to be 'shoehorned' into a traditional subject, such as English. 'The media' are not a separate part of our experience, as can be demonstrated whenever you ask anyone to define the term. (Try it with several people, and see whether you get the same list each time.) They are inextricably bound up with the whole complex web of ways in which we share understandings about the world, a web which includes gestures, jokes and hairstyles as well as news bulletins, opera and architecture; books as well as television. Like many people, I use the term 'culture' to cover all this. My starting point for this book is to suggest that, by admitting considerations of 'the media' into curricula – indeed, into the National Curriculum – an initial step has been taken in the direction of radically rethinking how we teach about culture. Or perhaps even more simply, a step has been taken towards acknowledging that we *do* teach about culture in schools, not just about the bits of it that fit into certain subjects. I will argue that we don't need any more checklists of curriculum areas or appropriate study objects, but we do need a conceptual framework that will enable children to learn, enjoyably and purposefully, about any and every aspect of their current, and potential, cultural experience.

However, the word 'culture' is another semantic hot potato and its connotations need to be explored before I can deploy it in argument. It can connote a world-view that sees culture, and in particular, education about culture, as essentially concerned with the preservation of league tables to separate great works from trash. There's nothing wrong with cultural league tables in themselves: most of us have got several, and enjoy arguing about them ('You mean to tell me you've never seen *Neighbours*/ read *Middlemarch*/ heard Ry Cooder? I can't believe it!'). But everyone's cultural choices and preferences are varied, undergo change, alter according to circumstance, and can never be contained in a pre-set formula. To believe that a certain set of league tables can be preserved for all time and taught to children as 'our cultural heritage' presents teachers – and children – with an all too familiar set of problems. A canon of great works can be used as an instrument of oppression.

Acknowledging these problems doesn't get rid of a residual anxiety, though. Isn't there always a risk that 'bad' will drive out 'good'? Isn't reading the *Sun* and watching soap operas easier, for most people, than reading Dickens or going out to see a Shakespeare play? Don't teachers have a responsibility to hand on the culture of the past? The answer to all these questions for most people is probably 'yes', but that doesn't tell us how to teach about culture, and indeed, it confuses the issue of what is meant by 'culture'.

In arguments of this kind, it often turns out that some people only mean established art forms like literature or classical music when they say 'culture', while others (like me) are using a much broader definition to include everyone's creative and communicative experience. The difference between these definitions is more than one of scale. Each carries with it sets of assumptions about society. The first, 'high culture', definition is essentially hierarchical: 'culture' is what you know about if you're 'cultured'; 'mass culture' is another, less worthy phenomenon, belonging to the undifferentiated 'mass' of the people. There's always a vulnerable audience out there somewhere (children, the less educated; in older scenarios, women and servants) which is likely to be seduced or manipulated by biased or meretricious texts. In this scheme of things, the value of cultural products enables you to put them on a universal scale: books or plays are given a value in relation to other books and plays; both books and plays are assumed to be of more value than television programmes or comics.

The second definition of 'culture' is not really concerned with putting books and plays, or comics, or home videos, into a universal scale of cultural values, but with valuing how people relate to their cultural experience. What pleasures and understandings do I get from this television series or that poem? How, and why, are they similar to or different from yours, or theirs? What might affect someone's choice of this book rather than that one? What access does each of us have to ways of sharing our ideas or communicating information to other people? Who controls the political information we receive and how do we get it? Within the terms of this definition, it is possible to think about books and television programmes, films and newspapers, as part of a totality. It's less easy to think about one medium (books, for example, or television) as requiring a special sort of attention and a special sort of education. It becomes important to put people, and their individual and common experiences, at the centre of the frame and to recognise that everyone operates many scales of cultural values and has many kinds of cultural experience. This way of thinking about culture has become more widespread as modern media such as television have become an increasingly significant part of our lives. It has led many teachers to question the kind of education about culture that goes on in schools, whether this is in the context of English, Art, Drama, Music, or even History and Geography.

Arguments like this always underpin most educational debate. Are we training children in traditional values, or are we forcing an outdated world-view on them? Does the curriculum really take account of people's experiences today and in the future, or is it harking back to the way things used to be? Are we valuing established curriculum content (and, perhaps, our own careers and departments) regardless of who's going to learn it, and why, and how? Most 'traditional' subjects in the present curriculum were established over the dead bodies of die-hard adherents of even older traditions, and new subjects fight the same battles. But rethinking the term 'culture' in the way I have described could have profound implications for education. It has to mean admitting new study objects to the curriculum, but it also ought to mean dividing up the curriculum differently. For example, all the traditional subjects that deal with expression and communication (English, Art, Music, Drama, and perhaps Modern Languages) might be grouped together as one subject, called – what? 'Communication Arts'? 'Rhetoric'? Perhaps even 'Media'? And since the list of what could be included under this heading would be impossibly long, it would be necessary to devise conceptual frameworks for learning: types of knowledge and understanding rather than lists of things to be studied.

Such things are not likely to happen at a time when new national curricula are being established in many countries, and the 'traditional values' arguments are being heard louder than ever. This is to be expected at a time of huge change and insecurity all over the world, even though, ironically enough, much of this change and insecurity can be attributed to the fact that the world's population is going through the biggest cultural upheaval in history, with more information, more stories, and more advice and opinion in circulation than ever before, thanks to media technologies. Nevertheless, educators and their political masters are beginning to realise that they have to do something about 'the media'. So the planners of new and revised national curricula in many countries, including England and Wales, are being charged with the requirement to include 'the media' somewhere in their proposals, while at the same time maintaining traditional curricular structures.

The result is usually that 'the media' get tacked on to national curricula somewhere, as part of mother-tongue teaching, or as an aspect of Information Technology, or as an optional bit of personal and social education, or citizenship, or something similar. But there is usually little guidance on what is meant by 'the media' or what the objectives of media education should be. Into this gap rush pragmatic definitions of the media, drawing on currently popular 'common sense'. Thus 'the media' are whatever people are thought to be anxious about in their children's cultural environment: they're what make children violent, or sexist, or racist, or hyperactive, or sleepy, or passive, or unable to concentrate (or several of these). 'The media' are what children spend more time consuming than they spend in school. 'The media' impair children's capacity to appreciate more valuable aspects of culture, like literature, theatre, or even live sport. 'The media' are what fill people's heads with right-wing ideas. Or left-wing ideas. It is interesting that right across the political spectrum there is a devout belief in the amazing powers of 'the media' to brainwash millions, in spite of an increasing volume of research findings suggesting that the relationship between 'the media' and their audiences is at least a little more complicated than simple cause-and-effect. Based on this kind of rhetoric, media education can be supported by both radicals and conservatives in the pious hope that it will lead to cultural and perhaps even social transformation.

After the rhetorical arguments have been made, planning for media education tends to run into demarcation difficulties. Does 'the media' really just mean television and the press? Are films a medium or an art form, or are they just part of television? Are television and video the same thing? How does popular music fit in? Is it worth including radio? Is advertising a medium? What about telephones? And how on earth can we fit all this into the curriculum? Faced with yet another list of things they ought to be teaching about, teachers' most positive first response is just to do 'media' themes and projects now and again. Or they may very well feel imposed upon, consider themselves unqualified to deal with a new area, and decide to leave it to someone else. One way or another, media education becomes a separate area, a separate set of technologies and study objects that are somehow different from books and children's own art or written work, and for which you somehow have to (or may refuse to) find time, energy and money.

In the United Kingdom's three educational systems, Scotland and Northern Ireland now have optional elements of media education in secondary schools, and England and Wales have a statutory requirement to study the media from Key Stage 2 onwards in the National Curriculum Statements of Attainment and Programmes of Study for English. Important though these curricular developments are, they all display to some extent the vagueness and confusions I have described. In this book I offer some ways of beginning to think about and plan for media education in the primary and lower secondary school (Key Stages 1 to 3). My main purpose has not been to offer classroom or INSET activities – although you may be able to derive some from what I have written – but to describe a conceptual framework through which you may be able to structure your own ideas. In writing the book I have drawn to some extent on my own classroom experience, but much more on the imagination and enthusiasm of the many teachers who already believe that good media education is an entitlement for all children.

CHAPTER 2

'Reading' Texts

At one level there are no photographs which can be denied. All photographs have the status of fact. What has to be examined is in what way photography can and cannot give meaning to facts.
(John Berger, *Another Way of Telling*)

In Chapter 1, I used the term 'text' apparently indiscriminately to refer to things that are often thought to be very different: television programmes, poems, photographs, newspaper items. Although 'text' usually means something written or printed, it is beginning to be accepted, even in the National Curriculum, as an abstraction referring to communications recorded in any form, whether print, audio or visual. It becomes increasingly important to have such a term when you are trying to establish a conceptual framework that will deal in the same way with many different kinds of . . . well, text. This sometimes leads people to think that media education has some kind of senselessly egalitarian or modishly post-modernist mission to make everything exactly the same; that it becomes irrelevant to distinguish between *Antony and Cleopatra* and a chewing gum wrapper – they're both texts. This is only half true. It can be interesting to compare wildly different texts through media education concepts, but the same concepts also lead you into identifying and accounting for their differences.

The first paragraph of this book invited you to think about the relationship between a writer and a reader and the processes that stand between them. Something like that paragraph could probably be written about the relationship between the producers, the audience and a text in any medium: film, television, photography, radio, the press. You could test this out by switching on the television at random for two or three minutes and then asking yourself the kinds of question you might ask about a book you'd glanced at: 'what encouraged me to go on watching?' or 'what made me want to switch off?' Having done that, you could then try to identify the factors that contributed to your answer. You were probably able to categorise the programme in some way, by recognising its style, content or the people in it. You were probably able to recognise the elements of the programme that its producers thought would appeal to you – even if they didn't. You may have become caught up in a fictional narrative or a factual exposition that aroused your curiosity, or you may have found these so predictable that you anticipated boredom at once. You may have been angered, pleased or intrigued by the way that the programme represented an event, a place or a social group; you may have made judgements about its accuracy, authenticity or degree of realism. Whatever happened, you were able to bring your knowledge and skills as a 'reader' of television to bear upon the experience, just as, in deciding whether to go on reading a book, you use your knowledge and skills as a reader of books.

However, this is not to say that switching on the television is the same as glancing at a book. The technologies that put them within your reach are different, with the result that you not only need different sets of skills to 'read' them but you also use them differently. You are probably reading this page by yourself, at your own pace; you could have watched your brief extract of television with others, in which case you would all have 'read' it at the same speed, although you would not necessarily all have reacted in the same way. You could carry this book somewhere else and read it there; televisions are usually much less portable. It is possible that your television extract was 'live': that it was showing you something happening at that very moment; a book can't do this.

The economic relationship between you and the producers of television programmes is also different from the relationship between you and a book publisher. Publishers want to sell copies of books. Television producers don't want to sell television sets, or copies of programmes. However they do, like publishers, want to ensure that they stay in business. They do this by making programmes that are watched by enough people – or, enough of the right category of people – to attract advertising. If they are producers in the public service sector of television, then their economic relationship with you is less direct, but still has an economic factor: licence fees pay for the BBC.

Lastly, and probably most obviously, the 'language' of each medium is different. You know that you must have been taught how to read the complex sign system of printed words; you probably don't have much sense of having learned to read the codes and conventions of television (although you may remember watching things you didn't understand).

It may have started to become clear from this comparison that it is precisely the process of applying the same considerations to different media that encourages us to identify characteristics specific to each that we might not otherwise have thought about. You could explore this further by considering two other texts (this time, visual images), and applying to each one the questions that could have been used to generate the comments I made in the last two paragraphs. The questions are in three groups, for reasons that will become clear later.

- What can you see here?
- What kind of image is it?
- What does it mean to you?

- How was the image produced?
- By whom, and why, was it produced?
- For whom was it made?
- How would it have reached its audience?

- Is it meant to be realistic?
- What does it represent to you?

In offering my own commentary on the images opposite, perhaps the most important point to make is that many of my observations may differ from yours. In some cases this may be because I have access to more information about the images than you do, but in other cases it will be because you bring experiences and ideas to the images that are different from mine. It's also possible that you may know much *more* about one or both of the images than I do. I should also point out that in neither case am I looking at the same image as you are. For me, Figure 1 is a colour postcard that I chose and bought from the National Portrait Gallery; Figure 2 is a somewhat creased and torn newsprint photograph that I cut out of a newspaper. For you, they are both black-and-white images printed in a book. These factors make a difference to what we can say about them.

What can you see here? What kind of image is it? What does it mean to you?

Figure 1 shows a full-length figure of a white woman in a long white dress with a very full skirt, tight bodice and full long sleeves. She also has a gauzy ruff and collar, and a cloak. The dress and her hair are decorated with jewels. She holds a closed fan in her right hand and a glove in her left. She is standing up, facing to the front and turned a little to her right. Her mouth is closed and her eyes meet those of the viewer. She is standing on a map. Behind her there is cloudy sky: to her left it is dark and

Figure 1

Figure 2

thundery; to her right it is sunlit. There is one line of writing on the left-hand side of the picture, and sixteen lines on the right-hand side, fourteen of which are close together and enclosed in a decorative frame. So far, there is probably a good deal of common ground shared by anyone looking at this image. From the colour print I can add that the jewels are red and gold, the cord holding the fan is orange, the woman's hair is reddish-gold, the glove is yellow and brown, the map various tones of green and buff, and the sky ranges from greeny-blue through yellow and brown to almost black.

You may very well be able to bring your own cultural knowledge to this image, and be able to say that it is an oil painting, that the dress is in the Tudor style, and that the woman is Queen Elizabeth I of England. You may recognise it as a portrait of her when she was older; you may indeed know it as a reproduction of the 'Ditchley' portrait, painted by Marcus Gheeraerts the Younger, probably in about 1592; you may have seen the original in the National Portrait Gallery in London.

The meanings this image has for you may well be very different from those it has for me. I am stunned by the detail of the clothing, curious about the shape of the body inside it, fascinated by the face of this woman (who was nearly sixty), uncertain about its relation to the real woman, intimidated by the power and confidence the image asserts. I have found out from reading about it that the white dress symbolised chastity to the Elizabethans and white was fashionable in the Tudor court of the 1590s; that the background suggests that the monarch could control the elements, 'her very presence banishing storms and ushering in sunshine' (Roy Strong, *Gloriana: The Portraits of Queen Elizabeth I*; Thames and Hudson, 1987, p. 138); that her position on the map relates to the location of the original owner's manor house in Oxfordshire.

Figure 2 shows a white woman, from the hips upwards, in profile, with her right arm stretched forward and one finger pointing towards the left-hand edge of the picture. Her left hand rests on her hip and her elbow is sticking out; her shoulders are rounded, her body flexed back from the waist, and her head is bent forward; she is looking along the line of her outstretched arm. Her hair is blonde and curly; she is wearing a white bustier or bra with pointed conical cups, and some sort of white belt or straps round her waist. Her mouth is slightly open. On the right-hand side of the image someone else's forearm and hand are pointing in the same direction, but lower. The background is completely black, with a few white patches towards the top.

Again, your own cultural knowledge will probably supply the information that this is a photograph and perhaps that the woman is Madonna, an American star of popular music and cinema in the 1980s and 90s. You may deduce from the costume that the photograph was taken at her July 1990 concert at Wembley Stadium, and from her posture, and the microphone that can be seen just above her right shoulder, that she was singing when the photograph was taken. You may deduce, or recall, that the photograph was reproduced in the *Guardian* the day after the concert (July 21st 1990).

Because this is a contemporary image, personal responses may be much more idiosyncratic. I happen to like Madonna and the knowing way that she plays with stereotypes; I like the way this image shows the muscles and veins in her arms and the assertiveness of her stance; I am startled by her resemblance to Marilyn Monroe but intrigued by the way she has appropriated and worked on Monroe's image; I am intimidated by her aggressive style but also admire it. I like the starkness and drama of this particular image. Your response may be very different.

How was the image produced?
By whom, and why, was it produced? For whom was it made?
How would it have reached its audience?

Although most people would be able to identify the original of Figure 1 as an oil painting and that of Figure 2 as a photograph, the processes by which they have both reached you make the answers to these questions potentially more complicated. What you have in front of you on page 11 was chosen by me and reproduced by Hodder and Stoughton, for a whole number of reasons including making a profit. Both images have been rephotographed through a dot-screen in order to make lithographic plates from which to print, and this changes the quality of the image. Before that, versions of the images were produced by the National Portrait Gallery and by the *Guardian*, in part at least because they were calculated to appeal to people like me and make a profit for those institutions.

Before that, in the case of Figure 1, we could go back through the history of the 'Ditchley' portrait to Sir Henry Lee, the owner of Ditchley House and the author of the sonnet that forms part of the painting, and the young, second-generation Dutch immigrant painter Gheeraerts. It could also be set in the context

What happens to Image where they originate.

of the sixteenth-century cult of images of the Queen, in which ownership of a portrait expressed one's loyalty to the monarch and the English Protestant state, and in which the portraits themselves expressed the sacred role of the monarch, her power and her virtue. Further investigation could go into the techniques of painting in oils on wooden boards, the colours and processes that were available to Gheeraerts, and the Renaissance style of painting that he was trained in, which used perspective and shadow in ways unfamiliar to the Elizabethan court and which displeased the Queen as showing her age too obviously. The portrait would have taken several months to produce, only a little of which time would have involved live sittings.

Again, it is not very hard to find out that Figure 2 was a commissioned image, taken by Alan Reevell, a freelance photographer who is regularly employed by the *Guardian*. Reevell was sent to the Madonna concert by Eamonn McCabe, the paper's picture editor, because the concert was seen as a major cultural event and another moment in the development of Madonna as a cult figure world-wide, and it would probably be important to feature it on the paper's arts page. Along with some twenty other photographers, Reevell was allocated a position to the side of the Wembley stage for the first fifteen minutes of the concert. He had to use a fast film (Fuji Neopan 1600) because concert administrators do not allow flash photography, a fast exposure (250th sec) to catch the moving figure, and a 200 mm lens to give the illusion of being near to the singer although he was ten metres away from her. Of the eighty photographs that Reevell took, this one was selected by McCabe for the front page as a powerful image that would attract attention.

Not enough is known about the 'Ditchley' portrait or Elizabethan portraiture in general to answer accurately the questions about audiences. We know that such portraits were an important political instrument in the sixteenth century in maintaining the power of the monarchy. They can in a sense be regarded as significant media texts of their time: one of the few ways in which what the Queen and her government felt to be the important information about the monarch and indeed the kingdom could be circulated to their subjects. Major portraits taken from life, as this one was, formed the basis for many copies both in oils and in engravings; the latter could be reproduced more cheaply, both in books and as single printed copies to be sold in the streets. But this particular portrait probably hung in the gallery of the newly built Ditchley House and was seen by other members of the Court, since Lee had until 1592 been the Queen's Champion (organiser of pageantry at Court). Since the 1590s, of course, it has been seen by many more people, especially after it was bequeathed to the National Portrait Gallery in 1932; it is now seen by most of the 625,000 people who go to the National Portrait Gallery every year, as well as being reproduced in hundreds of books, leaflets and postcards. Gheeraerts' own studio also made many copies of the portrait during the 1590s, some of which can now be seen in other galleries.

The Madonna photograph has in a sense two, overlapping audiences. One is the *Guardian* readers for whom the image was judged an appropriate item for the news-dominated front page; the other is the fans of Madonna. For both audiences the photograph becomes part of the way the 'image' of Madonna continues to be created and developed: photographic images, like royal portraits, play a crucial part in maintaining the power of the person portrayed. This particular image reached its newspaper audience through the established system of selection, editing, page layout, printing of 417,000 copies and distribution to retail outlets. The vast majority of these copies will by now have been thrown away, but many may be kept by Madonna fans. Unlike Gheeraerts, neither the *Guardian* nor Alan Reevell can make further use of the Madonna picture without permission from Sire records who control the circulation of Madonna images. Of course, both images are now circulating in a form unforeseen by their producers or previous owners: as part of this book.

Is it meant to be realistic? What does it represent to you?

Whereas the previous questions have relied to some extent on the evidence in front of you or the knowledge that you brought to it, these questions rely much more on your own judgement about the images. It's important to note that the first question does not ask 'is it realistic?' but 'is it *meant* to be realistic?' – in other words asking you to make a judgement about the producer's intentions. Both questions may also be more difficult to answer. At a very simple level, we can say that because Figure 1 is a painting, it was subject to Gheeraerts' interpretation of what he saw. Because Figure 2 is a photograph, we know that it has been made via a chemical reaction to the light and shadow that were in front of the lens, so that it is in some sense a more direct record of a specific moment in time.

In fact, we can deduce from the evidence in the painting that it was not intended to represent any specific moment in time. The map, and the fact that it seems to be part of a globe; the sky divided into sun and storm; the sonnet in its cartouche, all tell us that this image is allegorical: rather than a person in a real place at an actual moment in time, it represents ideas about that person and her role. In contrast, the appearance of the Madonna photograph on the front page of a newspaper guarantees for most of us that it was taken the day before, because that is what newspaper photographs usually are. Together with its caption: 'Pointed performance . . . Madonna at Wembley Stadium last night, in the opening show of the British section of her Blond Ambition tour' we are assured that this *is* a real person in a real place, and this is an important part of the meaning of the image. And yet, in the terms of our culture now, there is a sense in which the appearance of a rock star in her latest concert on the front page of a 'serious' newspaper *also* invokes ideas about that person and her role that are current in our society.

But judgements about levels of realism in any text are always more complicated than this. It might be argued that the Madonna photograph is grotesquely posed, that she is made up, dressed and lit in ways that make this image bear little resemblance to the real person. Likewise, the painting of Queen Elizabeth could be seen as a grotesque distortion of the real woman to fit the conventions of the pose and the costume. Yet it is also clearly an important part of the painting's project to represent that costume in extreme detail: the jewels, the embroidery and the fabrics are painted so that we can see their texture and solidity. And if we compare this painting with others of the same woman, we can see that in this one the face appears to be far less stylised, with shadows around the eyes and cheeks; it can be seen as exemplifying a new style of painting which was emerging in England in the 1590s and which tends to be judged as more realistic than earlier styles in portraiture. If we judge the Madonna picture against other types of contemporary photographs, we might well be struck by how flat and textureless this image is, compared with the minute details of skin, hair and fabric that we know can be shown in photography. But because we don't expect these in a newspaper photograph, and because such photographs offer us other guarantees of authenticity, we tend to judge them as 'realistic'.

So far, these comments have all been concerned with the way the images seem to relate to the actual people they represent.

But you might also judge them as being representative of certain kinds of people, groups or states of affairs. For you, a portrait of Queen Elizabeth may represent royalty, tradition, history, power, imperialism, or oppression. A photograph of Madonna may represent aggressive sexuality, liberation, power, depravity, blasphemy. Thus it may be possible to see each image as having potential ideological effects. This might be strengthened when you see the pictures juxtaposed, as they are here. To me they both seem to represent powerful women for whom the circulation of visual images was an essential part of maintaining their power, even though the nature of their power was rather different. In a book about media education, they also seemed an interesting way for *me* to represent the idea that 'media' have always existed and that technolgical or temporal differences don't necessarily lead to different kinds of critical analysis.

▬ *Summary* ▬

So far I have considered three main aspects of these images. Firstly, how the images may be (and may have been) understood and interpreted; secondly, how they were (and continue to be) produced and circulated to audiences; thirdly, the different ways in which they can be seen as representing reality, and ideas about that reality.

I shall return to these three aspects several times in this book. They are the same as the three approaches that are outlined in the Non-Statutory Guidance for English, issued by the National Curriculum Council in July 1990. In other books on media education you are likely to come across different approaches, key concepts, areas of knowledge and understanding. But they all draw on much the same theories and have developed out of the same academic traditions: cultural studies, structuralist literary theory, and sociology. For the purposes of starting media education in the classroom, it seems best to identify three broad aspects through which you can approach media texts. These should enable you to start to build you own conceptual framework and thus to be more confident about your aims and objectives in teaching about the media. Below, I list them together with more generalised versions of the kinds of question that relate to each one, and a brief summary of what each aspect includes.

Media languages

- What does this text say?
- How does it say it?
- What sort of text is it?

There is an underlying assumption here that each medium has at least to some extent its *own language*. These questions concentrate on the text itself and encourage you to consider *what* sense you make of it and *how* you make sense of it, by looking closely first of all at what is actually in the text. This could be the parts of an image (as in this chapter) but it could also be the way words, music or sounds are combined with each other or with images, the way images are combined with each other, and so on. Your assessment of the kind of text it is, and hence your expectations of it, will make a difference to how you read and interpret this language.

Producers and audiences

- How was the text produced?
- By whom, and why, was it produced?
- For whom was it produced?
- How did it reach its audiences?

These questions encourage you to look both within and beyond the text to the ways in which it was produced, circulated and received. Any text is part of economic, social, political and cultural systems, any or all of which can play some kind of role in determining what it means, what it can and cannot say, whom it can reach, and how it is valued.

Representation

- What judgements do you make about the truth/authenticity/accuracy/realism/effectivity of this text?
- What judgements might other people/groups make?
- What can it be said to represent?

This aspect concentrates on the relationship between the text and the things, people or events it is representing, and the judgements that can be made about that relationship. These could range from recognising the comic or fantastic intent of a text and modifying one's response accordingly, to identifying bias or stereotyping and being shocked, or dismissive of it.

CHAPTER 3

'Reading' Texts in the Classroom

What annoys me about the News is the way that it is put together. First they tell you about what they will be telling you about, then they tell you about some of it, then they tell you about what they have still to tell you about, then they tell you about that, and finally they tell you about what they've just told you about.

(Jane Bentley, aged 15, quoted in
One Day in the Life of Television)

If you are a teacher, you already use texts in the classroom with your pupils. The room, or rooms, that you work in already contain a wide range of texts: pictures, posters, books, worksheets, children's writing and art work, and quite possibly newspapers, sets of slides, audio tapes and video tapes. It is less likely but not impossible, that you may have a reel or two of Super 8 mm film or 16 mm film lying around as well. So since the National Curriculum now requires you to introduce your pupils to 'a range of media texts' (PoS for Reading, 18) does this mean that you carry on as you are, or not? The word 'range' is so vague – probably deliberately – that it could mean anything. Whereas the Programmes of Study for Reading give a good deal of guidance on the kinds of written texts you should be using, the guidance for other media simply makes occasional mention of 'television programmes' and 'radio'. Film and video aren't mentioned, but the pervasive use of the word 'text', together with the Non-Statutory Guidance declaration that 'text' is meant to be interpreted broadly (NSG p. D2, para. 1.10), effectively lays the onus on you to decide what you want 'range' to mean. In this chapter I will outline some ways in which you might think about this decision, and at the end of the chapter I will outline some ways of discussing media texts with children, based on the aspects I outlined in Chapter 2.

The National Curriculum guidance is symptomatic of the way non-print media tend to be classified in our culture. 'Print' is hardly ever used as a category: we talk about newspapers, novels, junk mail, magazines, information books, leaflets, posters, each of which conjures up in our minds a different kind of text with a different relationship to its audience. And yet 'television', 'cinema' and 'radio', which are also, like 'print', essentially technological definitions, are used as though their contents were all pretty much the same and were used in the same way. In fact each of these media produces a range of texts which is almost as wide as that of print, and addresses as wide a range of audiences. It would be an understandable, but unfortunate, result of the National Curriculum's vagueness if teachers interpreted 'a range of media texts' to mean 'a range of media technologies' and simply made sure that their pupils watched an educational television programme once in a while or listened to a poem read on the radio. There's nothing wrong with either of these activities, but they hardly constitute 'being introduced to a range of media texts'.

Once it is accepted that every medium produces a wide variety of texts, the cultural league tables I mentioned in Chapter 1 tend to come into operation. Although many teachers do not now operate a scale of acceptability in order to filter the texts that come into the classroom, many still believe, often rightly, that other people will. We all know the havoc that one outraged parent or a malignant local press can cause; the nightmare of PUPILS WATCH 'NEIGHBOURS' IN CLASS headlines haunts many a would-be media teacher. Nobody (apart from the occasional neanderthal 'no TV in my school' head teacher) has too much difficulty in accepting that it might be appropriate to watch television news in school, or to analyse advertisements from magazines. Most people think it's quite a good idea to see a Shakespeare adaptation on video or film now and again, or to watch the serialisation of a classic novel on television. Many people feel it's not unreasonable to show important television documentaries and plays in school. Relatively few people think that teachers have any obligation to analyse lager commercials, comics or Australian soap operas with their pupils. Hardly anyone thinks that game shows or Mills and Boon novels deserve curriculum space.

I would argue that cultural prejudices and assumptions have no role to play in deciding what texts do or do not come into the classroom. Each set of prejudices excludes or ignores aspects of cultural experience. 'High culture' prejudices exclude popular texts like game shows or soap operas. Proponents of popular culture may ignore European art cinema or avant-garde video. Ethnocentric assumptions about culture may exclude African cinema or bhangra music. Topical assumptions about 'our increasingly visual culture' may dismiss radio as unimportant. But all these – and many more – *could* be studied as a media text. The implications of this assertion in terms of the sheer number of texts you'd have to deal with are of course a real problem. This is where, again, it makes much better sense to be working within a conceptual framework, where you can set objectives of knowledge and understanding, rather than feeling overwhelmed by the mass of material you ought to be dealing with. You could consider your selection of texts under the headings of the three aspects I outlined in the previous chapter, using each one to generate your own questions about what kinds of media texts you could fruitfully be looking at in the classroom. These are not just questions that you have to answer as a precondition of media work. Your pupils could consider them too, and this would be part of media education. You might also want to work through these questions in an INSET or departmental planning context.

▬ *Media languages* ▬

- How many different media languages are there?
- Can we consider examples of each?
- How many different media categories or genres are there?
- What would be our criteria for selecting from these?

What does 'media language' mean? Looking across the main media forms, such as television, cinema, video, radio, publishing, and press, you might want to argue that each has in a sense its own distinctive way of making meaning. You could call these 'languages' or you could simply think of them as broad categories. In a slightly different and more literal sense, you might simply say that each of the major technologies, such as video, film, audio tape, photography and print, has a language of its own. Then there are other categories such as news or advertising, both of which appear in many different media. Genres are a huge and fascinating area of study. Some genres such as soap opera or science fiction also appear in more than one medium. Discovering and analysing the differences between all these – and discussing the problems about drawing boundaries between them – is a worthwhile activity in itself because it opens up all the complex ways in which your own (or your audience's) expectations and understandings are governed by the sort of text you are reading.

There are, of course, logistical, technical and financial considerations to bear in mind when attempting to look at range of media languages. These in turn bring us to the second aspect of media education.

© BBC

Figure 3 In what ways are these images similar and in what ways do they differ?

Producers and audiences

- What media texts do I and/or the pupils usually encounter?
- Who produces these texts?
- Where/how do we get access to them?
- How many different media circulation technologies are there?
- What types of media text do we like/dislike?
- What media texts do I and/or the pupils *not* usually encounter?
- Where/how might we get access to them?

How broad a range within each form could you realistically bring into the classroom? Do you have a responsibility to ensure that children get the experience of seeing films in a cinema rather than on video? Should you be ensuring that they do not just experience the dominant forms of broadcast television and the press, but are also able to discover independent, alternative and experimental work? Are there children of an ethnic minority in your class who could be sharing media texts from their own cultures with you and other children? Even if your class is not ethnically mixed, do you have a responsibility to make available texts from a broad range of cultures?

Obviously all of these questions may raise difficulties: how do you find out about texts that aren't widely available? What about language differences? Suppose the children wanted to bring in a violent video or a racist magazine? The point of the 'producers and audiences' aspect of media education is that each of these questions and worries is a teaching point in itself, and so are the consequent likes and dislikes, misunderstandings and objections. If you have valid reasons for excluding a text from the classroom, those reasons are themselves worth learning about. If the children enjoy a text that you don't, why is that? Classroom viewing and listening surveys are just a starting point for this area and should not only be used to establish what are the acceptable and accessible texts that everyone wants to study or make, but also to explore the very questions of acceptability and accessibility. A key issue in such discussions is likely to be judgements made by both you and the children in the broad area of 'representation'.

Figure 4 What is the target audience for this video, and how are the producers trying to appeal to it?

Of any selection of texts, can we:

- identify ones that are particularly significant for me/us/others?
- place them on a 'realism/fantasy' scale?
- place them on an 'offensive/acceptable' scale?
- suggest ideological roles any/all of them might play?

Any discussion of questions like these is fraught with potential difficulties. But as both you and the children build up experience of discussing media texts through all three aspects, issues about 'representation' should become contextualised and easier to handle. The answers to each of these questions are bound to link up with observations about what category of text is being discussed, how it is read, who made it and why, and how it has reached us. Unlike the questions relating to the other two aspects, these four are in ascending order of difficulty. Reception class children can talk about the texts they like and dislike, are frightened of or puzzled by, and can discuss levels of reality and fantasy, often using different criteria for each in relation to different texts. Junior children can begin to handle the shifting categories of offensiveness and acceptability, and hypothesise about the responses of people they don't actually know. Secondary pupils can explore the ways in which individual texts or aggregations of texts may have ideological effects depending on context and use.

'Fat Slags' from *Viz* (No. 43, Summer 1990)

Figure 5 Disgusting and offensive or self-confident and cheeky?

The important issue here as far as the selection of texts is concerned, is once again to look for breadth. Content analyses (how many pictures of women are there in today's papers, and what are they shown doing?) have a role here, but must form the basis of further questions. Where could there have been pictures of women and what should they have looked like? Can we accumulate a dossier of 'positive images' and consider where they might be seen? Is there such a thing as a 'positive image' or does it always depend on the context or the reader?

After all this, it may be a relief to learn that you could perfectly well start some media education work tomorrow by doing as I did for Chapter 2: cutting out an image from the paper that interests you, and starting to ask questions about it. Perhaps the most important disclaimer that needs to be set alongside the daunting range of media texts that you *could* be looking at in the classroom is: start small. In the face of teachers' prior disbelief, I have seen classes of seven year olds spend over an hour discussing one image or thirty seconds of television. What I wrote about the two images in Chapter 2 was only a fraction of what could have been said about them. The following extract from a taped discussion with four six year olds about a car crashing through a wall in *The A Team* illustrates the detail and concentration that are possible in such a session:

Sean	When they ducked down to go right through I thought they were just going to crash in – how can they open their eyes when they duck through, because all the dust would fall down on them, I thought . . . because it was in the other one that I saw it
CB	How do you mean, once they'd come through the wall they were all likely –
Sean	– to be cut
CB	I would have thought they would, really . . . I wonder if somebody can really do that; do you think they can?
Sean	Yeah
CB	Do you think people can really crash cars through walls and then . . .
Manisha	No, that was just um . . . um . . . not strong
Rezwan	. . . that was, that was just, that was just a tiny bit of plastic metal
CB	Plastic. OK. You interrupted Manisha, actually; let's hear what she was going to say . . . what was it?
Manisha	That was a . . . it was, um, a little bit, um, too, not, it wasn't really strong 'cause . . . but it was some what (*sound unclear here*)
Kelly	Uh? Miss, they're both black now (*looking at the tape spools*)

CB   OK, I'm just listening to what Manisha's saying

Manisha A little bit, um, was a little bit . . . that it was all plastic that, that, that the car could easily break, then, um, they covered it like, um, the plastic, a special plastic, they covered it in brown to make it look like wood

The issue of whether or not *The A Team* is an appropriate text to use in the classroom seems much less important here than the fact that Manisha is able to speculate at length about how illusions are created in a media text, and hence to extend her ideas about 'representation' as an aspect of understanding any text.

You might be the kind of teacher who likes to start with a big splurge: assembling a mass of materials brought in by both you and the pupils; discussing and categorising it all, reporting and presenting the results. There is much to be said for this and I wouldn't argue against it. But I still think that it is essential, when any group of children is starting media education for the first time, to do some close analysis of a very short or limited text, at some point early on in the work. This is because what you are teaching to start with is *another way of looking or listening*; one which will form the basis of all the subsequent work that you do. This is not to say that you are going against the grain or teaching children to think in a new and difficult way. Your first objective must always be to bring out the knowledge that children *already* have about media texts. I would hope that you didn't find the analysis in Chapter 2 very obscure or complicated, even though it may have drawn on unexpected areas of knowledge, or valued aspects of your knowledge differently. In Chapter 6, I discuss the importance of listening to children's talk about the media in order to identify and build on what they know. Many existing teaching materials (see Resources, pp. 60 – 61) show you ways of doing this kind of close analytical work at different age levels.

One starting point, then, could be the discussion of a pair of photographs as I did for Chapter 2, using the same questions. Your main problem here could be how you set this up in practical terms. Showing slides is the best way of ensuring that everyone in the class can see a high quality colour image; try using slides from another set of teaching materials. You could ask children to work in pairs on individual photographs, but this tends to lose the element of debate that in a whole-class discussion underlines the fact that images are open to a range of interpretations. If you can only work in this way, you could ask each pair to make an inventory of everything that is in the image, or to look at it for three minutes and then, when it has been removed, draw their own version. This at least encourages close observation of the image.

Don't just concentrate on still images, though. Tape a short television extract – an advertisement or a title sequence – and make a similar whole-class analysis, using the pause button (make sure the VCR has one) to stop and start. Cover the screen and listen to the sound-track (you could even do this to start with). List and discuss every element that you can see and hear, before jumping to conclusions about what it means or what it is for. It may well be that you don't all agree on what you see. Don't force a consensus. Above all, treat the whole exercise as a process of discovery, not only about the text, but also about the knowledge, skills and understanding that you – teacher or pupil – didn't know you had.

CHAPTER 4

Making Texts: Discovering the Language

> The heliographic method is at once *Democratic* and *Imperial*.
> Democratic because after a little simple trial and error, not to be
> compared with the labour of learning the painterly craft,
> excellent results may be secured by all. Imperial because it is a
> most voracious medium, which is capable of annexing the entire
> solid world and recreating it in two dimensions, instead of three.
> (Timothy Mo, *An Insular Possession*)

When we learn another language, many people find it easier to
listen to it or read it than to speak it. When they finally have to
say something, all kinds of obstacles and constraints appear,
some of them unexpected. It is not just a matter of mastering
the technical requirements of the grammar, but of knowing
current usage and idiom. Suddenly a simple utterance seems
enormously complicated and full of pitfalls. It seems much safer
not to try to be original, but to stick to banal observations out
of the phrase book.

Learning to use a media technology to express our own ideas
or communicate information puts us through the same sort of
process. This can apply to the very simplest technologies. There
are plenty of people who say 'I can't draw' or 'I'm no good at
writing', when confronted with the problem of translating their
thoughts into another medium with the help of a crayon or a pen
and some paper. Although we feel like experts in reading all the
products of media technologies that surround us all the time –
drawing, writing, photograhy, film, sound recording, computer
graphics – producing our *own* meanings in those technologies is
quite a different matter. Like the grammar, idiom and culture
of a foreign language, the accumulated expertise that lies behind
each technology seems colossal. And the more complex the
technology, the more extensive, esoteric and institutionalised
that expertise becomes. For this reason, any medium –
television, radio, cinema, press – should not be thought of simply
as a technology, but also as the institutional practices that have
accumulated around each technology: as, in fact, a language.

Adults are usually more aware of this than children. So

teachers who want to – or feel they ought to – embark on practical media work with children often find themselves in the curious position of being far less confident with the available technology than the children are. Given the economic and logistical arrangements in most schools, these teachers are also likely to be working under all kinds of stressful constraints – little equipment available, and what there is, available for only a limited time; little or no technical support; no assistance in the classroom. So what kind of practical media work can really be undertaken in the classroom? And what is the point of doing it, anyway?

This book is not a practical handbook: many of those exist already. But in this chapter I shall try to suggest ways in which you might set about answering those questions in your own teaching context. Although my definition of 'media' is a broad one, I shall place more emphasis here on audio-visual texts and technologies rather than print, since these are likely to be less familiar to you.

One useful starting point is to distinguish between media production and media practice. Media production is the process of making texts – photographs, video tapes, animated films, etc. – for showing to audiences. Media practice consists of exercises, some of them very limited and simple, that can be undertaken in the classroom and which help children – or you for that matter – to gain expertise and confidence with media technologies, and to explore other aspects of media such as representation, generic conventions or narrative structures.

Once you get beyond paper and pencil, access to audio-visual media technologies is usually limited. The temptation, or the pressure, is always to go straight into media production, whether in an INSET context or in the classroom itself. This should be resisted if possible. Everyone needs time to experiment with media technologies and find out what they can do. Whatever medium you are working in, you are always *translating* your thoughts into what you should think of as another language. You are bound to want to use technology in ways which are already familiar to you from your experience of that medium. If you are experimenting with video, for example, you will probably want to try out things you have seen on television, like interviews, advertisements, a scene from a soap opera or a police series. But you could also want to try out other ways of using the technology to say things of your own, especially as the equipment you have is likely to be very limited, and your audience, if you have one, will not be the same as the audience for broadcast television.

Even at this stage, it is useful to bear in mind the three aspects that I outlined in Chapter 2, as a way of structuring what you are doing and giving yourself a sense of direction. When you start to experiment with technologies, the most important aspect is likely to be 'media languages'. In a rather simple and basic sense, media technologies govern the ways in which things can be expressed, rather in the same way that the physiology of the human larynx and mouth mean that we make the sounds that we do and not the sounds that dolphins or birds can make. So you could ask yourself two basic questions:

- What can I say with this technology?
- What can't I say with it?

There are some obvious distinctions here, as far as audio-visual technologies are concerned. An audio recorder deals in sound only. A still camera doesn't give you moving images. But less obviously, especially to children, a video camera can give you moving images and sound instantaneously, while a film camera usually only gives you moving images and you have to wait for these to be processed. On the other hand, film images are of a higher quality than video, and are actually real photographs which can be seen on the strip of film, whereas video images are coded on to magnetic tape and cannot be seen on the tape. This means that the mechanics of editing film are much easier than those of editing video. However, editing sound tape is easier still – provided you have access to a reel-to-reel recorder. And so on.

The important point here is that finding out the potential and constraints of each technology can be a learning objective in itself. In an ideal world, children would be learning these in infant school at the same time as they learn the characteristics of pencil and pen, chalk and paint, chime bar and drum. Since we're not in an ideal world, you will simply have to take advantage of any opportunities for yourself, as well as the children, to discover what can be done with audio-visual technologies. INSET courses are a help, but it is also useful to find the time, if you can, to play and experiment with a camera or a tape recorder by yourself or in a small group. This in itself will give you ideas for how you can set up such activity in a classroom.

There are certain principles or elements of audio-visual languages that are common to several technologies and it is worth thinking about some of these and using them as a basis for practical exercises.

When you use any kind of camera, but also in any kind of two-dimensional art work, or any projected image, the frame is the boundary you choose for your image. It excludes what you don't want to show. It is thus a very important part of visual language. Remember that, just as words don't get on to a page by accident, you can control everything that is within the frame (except perhaps when you are taking fast action shots and you don't have time to compose your image). In a moving image, the way things or people enter and exit from the frame will be meaningful, and so will the way you move the frame across or through a scene. So, in framing an image through a viewfinder, you are making a *choice*, just as in writing you choose one word rather than another and thus make a difference to the meaning.

Exploring the choices involved in framing can be tried out as a classroom exercise. With a film or video camera set up on a tripod in the classroom, children can take it in turns to try out ways of showing the activity in the room, either by a series of shots or by swivelling the camera or tilting it up and down. If the camera has a zoom lens, they can try isolating individuals or groups. You don't need a film or tape in the camera to do this. Everyone takes a bit of time to get used to looking through a viewfinder, and some people, especially very young children, take quite a while to get used to controlling the movement of the camera and holding it steady, even when it is on a tripod. This can thus be an exercise that goes on informally while the rest of the class is getting on with other things. Alternatively, you can link a video camera to a television monitor so that the whole class can see what the person operating the camera can see. Everyone can then be involved in discussing different ways of framing the image and emphasising individual people or things.

You can formalise this exercise and structure it by sitting the children in a circle and have them pass an object from one to another round the circle, while each child has a turn at following with the camera each moment of exchange. This could be done with the monitor for everyone to see, or everyone could tape their own turn so that the class could view the whole exercise afterwards and discuss the techniques that had been used.

However, you don't need a moving-image camera, or even a camera at all, to experiment with framing. Still cameras without film in can be used by young children to get used to looking through a viewfinder. The very old box cameras with a big

(from the *Guardian* 8 October 1990)

Figure 6 In what ways do these two images differ? Try giving a different caption to each image.

square viewfinder on top are especially good for this. You can also cut a rectangle (say, 2″ × 3″) out of sheets of card for children to look through. If you can find a way of holding these frames steady in a position where children can draw what they see through the frame (taping them to the top of a chair back is one idea: each child then uses the chair seat as a table to do the drawing on) then the process of drawing *only* what you can see through the frame is a good way of developing the idea of the frame as a boundary. Of course, the frame doesn't have to be that shape or size; you could try out different ones.

Framing needn't involve looking through anything. You can experiment with changing the meaning of an image by 'reframing' photographs or drawings. Cut away or mask parts of an image, and see how the meaning changes. Show different parts of the image in sequence and see if you can make a story out of it. As a kind of reverse of this, you can stick images or parts of images on to large sheets of paper and ask the children to draw what they think is *outside* the frame.

▬ *Sequencing* ▬

Images and sounds can be placed in meaningful sequences in many media. A sequence of two or three still images can tell a story or express an idea, and often changing the order of the sequence can change the meaning.

Sequencing is a basic element of editing; perhaps the most important way in which you can control the meaning of a text. It is one of the greatest current drawbacks to practical media work in schools that it is virtually impossible for most children to have any experience of editing audio-visual texts. Trying out different ways of sequencing images is a limited way of compensating for this, but better than nothing. It is perfectly possible to splice film or audio tape in the classroom but getting access to the technology is likely to be a problem – even though the actual machines are quite simple. Editing video is much more complicated, although you can do a basic re-ordering of material by re-recording (or 'crash-editing') from one video recorder to another. You can do the same, more easily, from one audio cassette tape to another.

Because comics are cheap, teachers often use cut-up comic strips for children to try re-sequencing the images or even just putting

Figure 7 'Pandas and Humans' by Philip Sydney (Duxford School, Cambridge)

Figure 7a 'Toddlers United' by Tom Mustoe and Simon Howarth (Duxford School, Cambridge)

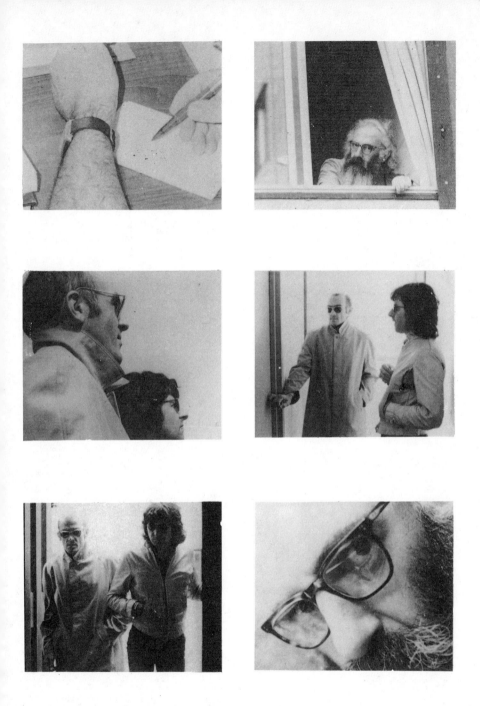

Figure 8 *The Visit: An Exercise in Suspense* (published by the English and Media Centre, London, and distributed by the National Association for the Teaching of English, Birley School Annexe, Fox Lane Site, Frecheville, Sheffield S12 4WY.)

Figure 8a *The Visit: An Exercise in Suspense.* What differences in the story are made possible by the rearrangement of these six images?

them in the right order. The problem is that many comic strip images are so simplified that you could put them in almost any order and make some sort of sense out of them, although they are useful for very simple sequencing work by infants. You should be encouraging juniors or secondary children to pay attention to everything in an image (as in the analysis in Chapter 2) as part of the process of making a sequence, so select – or get them to make – images that have some complexity. You will find that even in the reframing exercises with a single image that I described above, every image suggests narrative possibilities: 'When we find a photograph meaningful, we are lending it a past and a future' (John Berger, *Another Way of Telling*; Writers and Readers Publishing Cooperative, 1982).

Another exercise that some media teachers are very keen on is storyboarding. Children are asked to plan an audio-visual production by drawing in sequence the images that are supposed to appear in the finished film or video, often adding the dialogue or sound effects, or explanatory captions, underneath or at the side. Usually the teacher supplies a pre-drawn format of blank frames ready-printed on pages. Sometimes – for instance in planning an animated film or something that is very tightly constructed – storyboarding *is* essential. It is also important when children are working as a team and can use a series of pictures for reference more easily than they can a written script. But I doubt if it is always useful. The gap between the drawings – which some children may find a great struggle – and the immense possibilities of the real camera is enormous. Children should at least have a chance to practise looking through cardboard frames or a camera viewfinder before trying to do storyboarding.

Projection

This is a technological solution to the problem of how to show an image to many people at the same time. It precedes modern audio-visual technologies by several hundred years. Electronic and broadcast images may eventually overtake it, but at the moment it is still the basic arrangement of lenses, light and mirror that can provide the largest, sharpest and most brilliant images that are available to most audiences. The first time children see their own photographs or film projected on to a large screen is always a thrilling moment. It is also a simple and satisfying technology to play with in the classroom. Experiments with an overhead projector can reveal the characteristics of all kinds of materials under the light-and-magnification treatment. Is a paper tissue translucent? What shape are grains of sugar? How can you mix colours with light?

You can use this knowledge to *make* slides rather than photographing them. Buy glass-slide mounts and make drawings with OHP pens on tiny squares of clear or coloured acetate, or scratched on to blank exposed film. Or sandwich all kinds of materials between the two halves of the glass slide: ink, sugar, hair gel, lace, paper, cotton wool, hair, thread, scraps of metal foil and plastic, to make abstract images.

Sounds and images/words and images

There are four elements of sound recording: words, music, sound effects – and silence. Alone or in combination, they very often carry more of the meaning of an audio-visual text than the images do. Try listening to the television with the screen covered. Then watch television with the sound turned down. Which is more informative?

There is an over-emphasis in media education, and in our culture generally, on the significance of the visual. Yet you very rarely see images without hearing sound with them, or seeing words printed alongside them. There are many basic exercises in image analysis in media education that involve studying a picture and then trying out ways of changing its meaning by adding different captions; you could try this with any of the images in this book.

One relatively under-explored media form that is within the technological capacities of most schools is tape-slide: not a poor relation of video or film but a satisfying medium in its own right, using slide sequences and audio tape. You can start with a sound tape (music, a poem, a story, sound effects) and make slides to go with it, either by photography or with the glass-mount process I described above. Or you can start with the slides and devise a sound track to go with it. There is a simple gadget with which you can connect the tape player to the slide projector and code signals on to the tape so that it changes automatically. Amazing effects can be achieved with two or more slide projectors, fading or switching from one to the other (you can do this with your hands covering the lenses) or superimposing images.

In this chapter, I have described just a few of the immense number of ways that you can experiment with producing meanings through media practice; in other words, discovering media languages. Anyone who has gained some confidence and expertise in these languages is bound to want to see whether they can make something satisfactory for an audience.

CHAPTER 5

Making Texts: For Whom and Why?

> It is particularly striking that the act of writing was on occasions
> a means by which children actively rejected and embraced the
> overtly expressed principles of their upbringing and in this way
> came to comprehend and absorb an adult world of meaning at
> their own level of understanding.
>
> (Carolyn Steedman, *The Tidy House*)

Discovering media languages can be an exciting and liberating
process. But a great deal of writing about media work in schools
stops there. Media education becomes a series of fun things to
do, often justified in terms of the spin-off learning that it
generates in 'real' subjects like science, maths and technology.
There is a hazier notion that practice and production work in
audio-visual technologies actually fosters a critical understanding
of the media. This may in some senses be true, but it has hardly
been investigated. We need to be clear about why we want
children to make their own media texts and what we think the
outcomes may be, even if we have to revise these once such
practice becomes more widespread and has been more fully
considered.

'Producers and audiences', and 'representation', the other two
aspects of media education that I have already outlined, can help
to structure our thinking here. In this chapter, I shall offer some
ways of considering children's media production through these
two aspects. I shall therefore be concentrating on the process of
making texts for showing to audiences, rather than, as in the
previous chapter, on the 'classroom exercise' type of work that
I characterised as media practice. I shall not be offering practical
advice on how to set about media production in the classroom,
since to do that would be a book in itself (but see Resources,
pp. 60 – 61).

First of all I want to ask some basic questions. *Should* media
education include learning to 'speak' or 'write' the languages of
all the different media? To understand a language, both as a
listener/reader and as a speaker/writer, is to be empowered.
People who can communicate well have more power over their
own lives, and often over other people's also, than people who
can't communicate well. Knowing several languages is obviously

more empowering than knowing only one. But how realistic an aspiration is this? How many forms of communication have you learned? How many are taught in schools? How many could be taught?

These are not simple questions. Once the word 'language' is extended from its everyday meaning of 'verbal language' and applied to things like drawing or photography or radio, and we start to use terms like 'reading' pictures or 'writing' audio-visual texts, then the difficulties of persisting with this literal analogy become apparent. Many media educators – myself included – have used this analogy as a polemic: to argue that understanding and using audio-visual technologies ought to be taken as seriously as reading and writing verbal language. Hence we get terms like 'visual literacy' or 'media literacy'.

The force of this argument can depend very much on how the term 'literacy' is understood. It can be used to mean just 'basic competence', so that 'media literacy' can be used to mean a basic competence in, say, getting 'correct' understandings from television and mastering the technical procedures of taking a photograph. Chapter 2 began to show, I hope, how complex are the processes of understanding even one visual image, so it's hard to envisage what getting a 'correct' understanding of television might mean. Likewise, technical procedures are not all that's involved in taking a photograph, any more than writing consists solely of spelling and handwriting. In fact, 'basic' very often means 'uncritical', and calls up authoritarian models of teaching where technical competence comes first, and forming hypotheses and asking questions comes later.

There is also the problem of how literacy in reading is supposed to relate to literacy in writing. Do you have to have both to be literate? We'd probably all say yes, but in practice most of us are much better at reading than at writing – and do much more of it. Is there much of a relationship between what we read and what we write? It's interesting to reflect upon how these two aspects of literacy are taught about in schools. We are taught to read print, how to recognise different forms of published writing (novels, newspaper articles, information books etc.), how to find books in libraries, how to handle indices and encyclopaedias. But what we're taught to produce is handwriting. Granted, many schools now encourage children to produce forms of print such as word-processed and duplicated books, or school newspapers and magazines; but this is still unusual enough to be remarked upon. The National Curriculum requires competence in spelling and handwriting. There aren't any attainment targets for keyboard skills, sub-editing, page layout, print costing, binding techniques or calculating profit margins. Those are the professional skills of the publishing industry and are assumed to belong to vocational training.

Producers and audiences

By undertaking media production children probably do learn something about the professionally produced media texts that they see every day. But what they learn may well be highly dependent upon the way this process is handled in the classroom and what the teacher's motivation is. They may learn some of the 'rules' of professional production; they may learn to admire the skills of the professionals; they may learn to spot the operations of bias and manipulation. During such tasks teachers often feel that it is important to stress the analogies between the children's production procedures and those of media professionals. The tasks of 'editor' or 'director' are assigned to individuals or groups and the whole class pretends to be a newsroom or a film studio. But in the end, it makes as little sense to assert that children are making 'books' or 'newspapers' in school as it does to say that they're making 'television' when they produce a class video, or 'radio' when they tape an interview. This is not just a matter of the gap between the technical facilities in most classrooms and those of media institutions like publishers or broadcasters. It is more like the gap between me as a speaker of fairly simple basic French, and a literate Frenchwoman. It's not just that she knows much more grammar and vocabulary than I do, but that she has inhabited that culture all her life and knows how the language operates within it. The gap between a child with a camcorder in a fourth year junior class and, say, Roger Goss (currently camera supervisor on *EastEnders*) is not just that Goss has more expensive cameras and other technical facilities, but that he is an experienced professional working for a powerful institution.

These observations are not intended to crush teachers' and children's aspirations about their own media production. Quite the reverse. My view is that classroom media production ought not to be trying to pretend that there isn't a difference between the fourth year juniors and the BBC, but that one of its ultimate objectives should be an increased understanding *of* that difference. After all, there are other differences between the child with the camcorder and Roger Goss. The child can show things that Goss can't show, and can reach different audience groupings in different ways. Just as we don't expect children in school to write best-sellers, we don't have to confine children's media production to the imitation of dominant media forms like news, advertising or soap opera. They could be making video poems or satirical entertainment about the school, as well. The previous chapter has shown some ways in which media practice can develop children's sense of the potential of media technologies. When it comes to media production, children should first be learning about their own potential as media producers, just as they currently learn about their own potential as writers, musicians or painters.

However, there is another dimension to such learning, which tends to arise in the context of media education but should not, logically, be confined to it. If junior school children are, say, making a video about their school to be shown to prospective parents, they have to make some careful decisions about what should be shown and what should not be shown. They would have to guess, or find out, what parents think a good school is like and try to find images that would meet those expectations. They would have to meet the requirements of the Head and the governors, and might have to submit versions to them for approval. That process would teach them a great deal about the school as an institution and the processes through which decisions get made.

As children get older and gain wider social experience, they get a fuller sense of what is and isn't possible within different institutions. Of course, there are different ways of fostering this kind of understanding. It could easily be seen as a way of training young people for the job market; ensuring that they'll fit into their work place; encouraging them to believe that institutions are static and unchanging. Alternatively, it can be seen as a way of revealing to children how the power of the media operates: how governments or multinational corporations may try to control what can or cannot be said in the press or on television. Such understandings are certainly very important and an essential part of media education. But in my view, they are not enough. The ultimate aim of teaching children about media institutions should be to enable them to see where real innovation is achievable. It is surely frivolous to teach children to 'resist' stereotyping and bias, without also teaching them

practical ways in which counter-arguments might successfully be
made. What would be the point of encouraging children to
realise the creative possibilities of a medium without teaching
them where and how such possibilities might find expression?
Too much media education has set itself the limited objective of
getting children to resist media manipulation, without
encouraging them to find out how things might be different. So,
as well as learning about their own potential as media producers
– or, for that matter, as writers, musicians or painters – the
school surely has a responsibility to teach about the possibilities
for change and development that are open to professional
producers, rather than teaching about professional practice as a
set of givens. In the real world, change and development take
place within and between institutions. Children need to learn
about how this happens.

As producers of real texts, children also have to develop an
understanding of the audiences they might reach. The starting
point here is an understanding of themselves as members of
audiences. This includes understanding that audiences can be
people you don't know, and that anyone can be a member of
many different audience groupings. A black girl who enjoys soap
opera and football will sometimes be part of the same audience
as a white boy in the same class who enjoys soap opera and
country music, and sometimes not. But even when they are part
of the same audience, watching *Home and Away* or *Brookside*,
they may have different interpretations of the same text, that
relate to their ethnicity and gender. Knowing that texts are open
to different interpretations and that audiences bring meaning to
texts is not just a piece of specialist knowledge that teachers of
reading need to have, but an essential part of learning about how
texts work.

Developing an understanding of the concept of 'audience' is
one area that has become as important a part of English as it is
of media education; it is written into the Statements of
Attainment for writing from Key Stage Four onwards, in the
National Curriculum for England and Wales. However, the
effects of audience awareness only seem to be looked for within
the texts that children write: choosing appropriate structures and
vocabulary, for example. The idea that you also have to know
how your text is going to *reach* its audience is hardly considered,
even though this must be as important for writing as for any
other medium. If our video is for prospective parents, how are
we going to let them know about it? Should we advertise it in

the local nurseries and playgroups? Would we set up screenings or would we make copies of the tape to lend out? How much would that cost? Who would want to buy our class newspaper apart from our class? If we wanted to sell it to other people, what should we put in it to make it interesting to them? What would be the best technology to use in making copies, both in terms of what it would look like, how many copies we could make, and how much it would cost? Could we get people to advertise in it in order to cover the printing costs? How much should we charge for it? Questions like these should not be problematic afterthoughts in the production process, but planned for as learning objectives from the beginning. They are part of what it means to reach 'real' audiences.

▄▄ *Representation* ▄▄

Reaching real audiences means getting real responses. At this point, the issue of 'representation' also becomes real. Again, this is where a close relation between critical work on media texts and undertaking media production can have a positive effect on both. The complicated question of how realistic an image is turns into a practical issue of whether we can afford make-up and costumes, or what special effects we can achieve with this camera. Thinking about representation in relation to media production is closely bound up with the institutional issues I have discussed already. Any audio-visual production by children or young people that is addressed to real audiences has to confront the fact that it will be immediately identified as a 'children's production' or a 'school production' and may be admired, or dismissed, for that reason alone. Children should be encouraged to think about the potential advantages of this instant identification, rather than try to pretend it doesn't exist.

The reason why a great deal of media production by children takes the form of parody or fantasy is probably partly that it is trying to avoid this sort of identification; also we should not forget that parody and fantasy are more likely to be the media forms that children know and enjoy, than are news, documentary and current affairs. The reason for most children's enjoyment of film and television advertisements is not necessarily that they like the products, but because most of the best advertisements use parody and fantasy. It is often thought that our culture values realism, but in fact in many of our major cultural forms – cinema, for example, and, increasingly, literature – fantasy, horror, magic, comedy, romance and adventure are the ones enjoyed by the largest audiences. The cultural league tabling that puts realism at the top of the scale and ranges the rest below it (with horror and romance probably tying in last place) is fostered by education and, at least in Britain, by television, where realist drama and prestige documentary are still held in such high esteem. In this context realism seems almost to have some kind of moral authority, rather than being one amongst many possible modes of expression. It is bizarre that media education has concerned itself so much with non-fictional forms like news and advertising (an emphasis reproduced in the National Curriculum) when most of children's media experience lies elsewhere.

Stereotyping and bias are aspects of representation. We make judgements about them in relation to our ideas about possible or desirable representations. We tend to accept stereotyped or biased representations when they don't challenge our ideas about the world, or when they appear in generic forms that we know are not meant to be taken seriously, like cartoons or horror films. On the other hand, people make different judgements about stereotyping and bias according to their social group and their personal experience.

Criticising stereotypes and bias in media texts is a good theoretical exercise, but it is only part of learning about how they work. When it comes to media production, children are compelled to negotiate all the varied ways in which offence and anger can be caused. People who make sexist or racist remarks usually try to justify them by denying their general significance: 'I was just being friendly'; 'it was just a joke'; 'it didn't mean anything really'; 'you're just over-reacting'. They resist the idea that what they have said can be seen as part of a pattern that the recipient of the remark has learned to recognise as *systematic*; as symptomatic of a power structure that disadvantages them. In making media texts, children should be learning that they can control everything that goes into the text: every part of the image, every sound on the tape, every word on the page. They are also controlling what is *not* in the text; what is excluded from it. In their critical work on media texts, they should be developing their awareness that every bit of a text can be meaningful; can be 'read' by the audience; can be thought of as part of a system of codes and conventions.

All these factors have to play a role in how children make

their decisions about what does and does not get included in their text. In making a classroom-based news bulletin on video, the question of whether a black child rather than a white child is the newsreader might be discussed as a significant issue. Similarly, it could be a deliberate break with convention to have a girl doing the commentary in a video about the school sports day, given that the vast majority of sports commentators on radio and television are male. Planning a photo-documentary about the school should include discussions about bias and objectivity: squalid toilets or graffiti-covered walls might or might not be excluded, depending on the purpose of the text. Such questions are also relevant to discussions about how the texts themselves get made. Are the boys getting to use the camera more often than the girls? Is decision-making really shared or are one or two people having their own way all the time?

Confronting issues in this way may be difficult in the institutional culture of your school. Explicit discussion of how ethnicity is or is not going to be represented may conflict with the kind of anti-racist teaching that tries to insist that racism is something to be excluded and denied any place in the school. It could create embarrassment and problems for individual children. Media education does not have magic solutions to these difficulties. But by locating questions about stereotyping and bias within the broader area of representation, it at least offers you the possibility of encouraging children to think systematically about *all* the ways in which texts relate to reality, rather than just concentrating on the 'bad bits'.

■ *Conclusion* ■

This chapter has tried to show some of the issues that ought to be considered when children embark on media production. For me, the quantity and complexity of these issues raise two important questions.

Firstly, if media production work is really this complicated, what sort of classroom productions are really feasible? The answer here is to be much more modest in your production ambitions than you may originally have thought of being. Start small. The technology and time that are available to you, and the issues that have arisen in the course of critical work and media practice, will tend to dictate what kind of production you and the children want to do, but where there are decisions to be made about, say, the length of a video or the number of photographs to be taken, go for the lowest acceptable estimate. It may also be possible to build up a media text through the accumulation of short items made by individuals or small groups within the class: an animated film consisting of a series of 3- or 4-second shots, each made by a different group. Arbitrary constraints like allowing each person a maximum of three photographs or thirty seconds of audio tape can be constructive rather than limiting. You can also aim for a tighter focus of subject-matter. Almost any audio-visual production is heavily constrained by time and cost so you are not imposing something that professional producers don't have to work with. But the production situation for children is different from that of the professionals in that it is a much greater learning experience. Whenever possible, a production should not be seen as the end of a process but as a stage in learning; children will very often want to start again immediately, and try to do better; this should be anticipated.

Secondly, is there any logic that confines to audio-visual media the issues I have described in this chapter relating to children's production? I would say no. Some teachers and schools have already begun to address these issues in the context of children's writing or art work including performing arts, but it is certain that the ideas about institutions and about representation that I have outlined here are very rarely investigated in schools. I think they should be, and the experience of primary school teachers who have been able to start media teaching in a cross-curricular context bears this out: 'The more I taught media education, the more important it became as an attitude of critical awareness that underpinned all projects, and the less I saw it as a separate subject' (Dot Froggatt, 'The Lowry Project', *Media Education in Primary Schools 2*, Occasional Papers for Teachers of English in West Sussex, Horsham Professional Centre/BFI).

CHAPTER 6

Progress and Planning

They had overheard, or been told, or had read, at any rate
absorbed the idea that they, 'the inheritors of our future, etc etc',
were being fed a view of the world, life, that was all killing and
violence. Both had used this idea to attack the adult world: self-
consciously on stage, they had seen themselves as corrupted from
birth. The adults, agreeing with them wholeheartedly and at
once, had gone on to claim the same condition for themselves.
(Doris Lessing, *The Four-Gated City*)

Children inevitably learn *about* television – and other media –
as well as learning *from* them. By the time they arrive in school,
almost all children will have experienced several years of
television, and probably other media as well, such as radio, films
on video, and picture books. They will probably know what
newspapers and magazines are, even if they can't read them.
They may be familiar with story and information books, and
family snapshots, and will have seen hundreds of posters in
streets and shops. Even if they haven't talked about all these
media forms very much with their parents or siblings (although
it would be surprising if they hadn't) they will still have gained
some understanding of social and cultural attitudes to the media,
of different technological and generic forms, some hypotheses
about how real or true some texts are, and some skills with
operating media equipment, like stopping and rewinding a VCR,
or standing still for a camera. Media education can start as soon
as children arrive in school and, through both critical and
practical work, can build on the skills, knowledge and
understanding that children already have, using the conceptual
framework of 'media languages', 'producers and audiences', and
'representation'. It can continue throughout schooling,
developing alongside the media understandings that children
continue to gain outside school; it is one subject that *has* to
bridge the home-school gap.

At least, that's the theory. In practice, the curriculum is
overloaded, teachers don't have the experience or confidence to
undertake media work – especially practice or production – and
not even media teachers are clear about what a fully-developed
5–16 media curriculum might look like. There's a great deal of
research and development to be done. Nevertheless, an

increasing number of teachers are still going to start trying to teach about the media, either because they're interested and think it's important to do so, or because the National Curriculum tells them to. In this chapter, I shall try to suggest some ways in which you could make a start on media education, whether you teach in Key Stage 1, 2 or 3. At each stage, I will indicate how the things you could do relate to the three-part conceptual framework I have been describing in previous chapters. It is much more difficult to be specific about how media learning might progress from stage to stage, because so few children have had a consistent media education experience over a period of time, and there is therefore very little evidence to go on.

Key Stage 1

Media languages

Although we don't know nearly enough about the media knowledge that four and five year olds have gained, it is very likely that a lot of it underpins what they later learn in school. Most children's experience of narrative structures and story genres has been gained in watching television and video more than in listening to stories read aloud or told. Most five year olds have seen thousands more images of different kinds of people and different parts of the world, than five year olds did forty years ago.

In her book *Television is Good for Your Kids* (Hilary Shipman, 1989) Máire Messenger Davies gives a very helpful account of her own and other people's researches into how children make sense of film and television languages (pp. 19–26). She suggests that many four and five year olds are still learning the codes and conventions of audio-visual story-telling, and may still have a lot of difficulty in following an extended narrative. By the time they are seven, most children will be able to follow such stories and know what is meant by a close-up or by cross-cutting from one scene to another. By encouraging children to talk about these understandings as they develop, we may help this process along, but we will certainly, and perhaps more importantly, show children that these understandings are valued by the school.

Opportunities to play with media technologies should be sought and encouraged. Looking through cardboard frames and camera viewfinders, and talking about what can and cannot be seen at different distances and from different angles; experimenting with lenses, light and different forms of projection; trying out persistence of vision toys such as flicker books and zoetropes; these and similar activities form a basis for more extended work on media production. Looking at and talking about a wide range of texts will offer plenty of opportunity for thinking about and discussing how to categorise different types of text.

Producers and audiences

'My mum wouldn't let me watch it; it's too frightening.' 'That's just a little kids' programme.' 'I got my picture in the paper.' 'Why do they put that programme on so late?' 'They're only trying to make you buy it.' 'I wanted to see it but my Dad wanted to see the football.' 'I wonder how they did the bit where the man fell out of the helicopter.'

All these everyday remarks can be seen as expressing ideas about how media texts get produced and how they circulate to audiences. Who controls what you see, how texts affect audiences, who gets access to the media, the motivations of advertisers, the targeting of different audiences, the way producers create illusions, are all important issues, yet they crop up all the time in children's casual talk. You can respond to these kinds of remark in ways that encourage children to think through the issues. For instance, the word 'they' occurs several times in the comments I've quoted. Asking who 'they' are usually produces an interesting discussion.

Looking at or listening to the credits on television or radio programmes, or films, even if children cannot read yet, emphasises the number of people who may be involved in making media texts and can be related to children's own media production: how many people will have to help in making the video? Talk about choices and preferences in television programmes or other texts may crop up informally but is an important part of beginning to think about audiences and about how people's preferences and understandings may differ.

Representation

Much more important than stereotyping and bias to young children is the issue of how real or true media texts are. As Bob Hodge and David Tripp argue in their book *Children and Television* (Polity Press, 1986), perhaps the most important basis teachers can offer children in developing their ideas about representation is to ensure that they encounter texts that range right across the fantasy-reality continuum. Judgements about realism also lie behind most comments about 'frightening' or 'exciting' texts. Again, these issues are likely to emerge in everyday talk.

The starting point for media education in the infant school is listening, and responding, to children's talk. For INSET work, it is remarkably rewarding to record and transcribe children's talk about the media and really try to analyse what is going on. Even the process of transcription itself is a powerful learning experience for teachers (although it is much more time-consuming than you might think). The talk can relate to texts seen outside school, or to ones seen in the classroom, or to practical activities such as drawing, writing, making audio tapes, taking photographs or trying out the video camera.

━━ *Key Stage 2* ━━

The scope for media education in the junior school is enormous. Not only can you assume that most of the childrren can get at least some grasp of the basic concepts, and that they have the practical and social skills to undertake practice and production, but media work can play an important role in every part of the curriculum. You can take up this potential in different ways. You might feel that media education should simply permeate the curriculum, so that you never explicitly do 'media work', but you take care to develop the 'media' aspects of everything that you do. Or you might want to be sure that you did a media-led topic at least once a year.

Whether you take either option, or a mixture of both, you need to be clear about what you mean by 'media work' and how you are defining 'media'. I have argued in this book that 'media' should be seen in broad terms (i.e. as including reading and writing) and that it is the conceptual structure that matters. The logical conclusion of this argument is that there wouldn't really be such a thing as media education at all, but, as I argued in Chapter 1, a common and systematic approach to the 'reading' and production of all kinds of texts. However, if you consider that you or your school are not at that stage yet, it may be important for you to define 'media' conventionally as television, press, radio, film, etc; and it may be essential that you do explicit 'media' topics, in order to clarify for yourself, your pupils and your colleagues just what it is you are doing with these new study objects and production technologies.

As you gain experience in doing this, you will probably find it increasingly easy to see the links between the media topic and other areas of the curriculum. The danger here may be that people who are less familiar with the aims and approaches of media education will simply extol it as a jolly good way of doing *other* things, as in 'you can use media education to help with science'. This may be true, but it's also true that you can use science to help with media education. Children doing sound recording will simultaneously learn about aspects of *Science AT14, Sound and Music,* and about the possibilities of sound tape as a medium of communication and expression. Media education draws on other subjects, and in doing so, enriches them. It doesn't disappear into them.

As a kind of halfway house between the two options, here is a way of starting to plan a general topic for first year juniors that deliberately includes media elements.

Media education concepts applied in project plan

Media languages
- exploring visual narrative through ordering and reordering of cartoon pictures
- producing and interpreting meaning in different media – music, video cover, literature, cartoon, performance
- beginning to recognise codes and symbols in advertisements relating to fire

Producers and audiences
- identifying companies who use fire images in packaging and advertising, and considering why this is
- selecting features for video cover; considering where video would be placed in shop or library
- deciding in what sort(s) of newspaper the dragon stories would go
- where can images of dragons be found, and why?

Representation
- discussion about realism/fantasy in *Pete's Dragon* which mixes animation and live action
- how are princesses, St George, and dragons represented in various media: as heroes, victims, villains; as evil or good? identifying how these characteristics are shown
- how a mask can, or cannot, change you

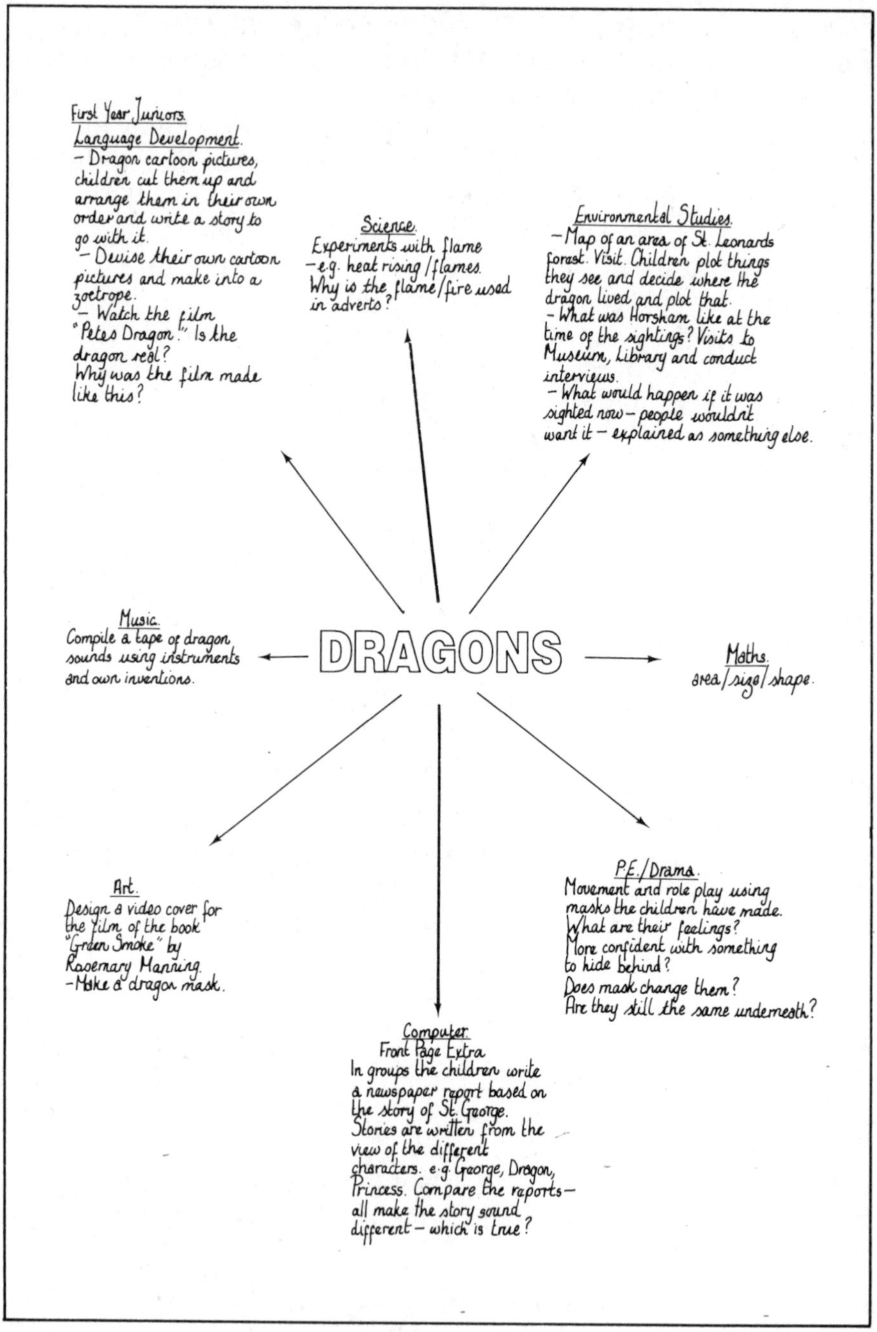

First Year Juniors.

Language Development.
– Dragon cartoon pictures, children cut them up and arrange them in their own order and write a story to go with it.
– Devise their own cartoon pictures and make into a zoetrope.
– Watch the film "Pete's Dragon." Is the dragon real? Why was the film made like this?

Science.
Experiments with flame – e.g. heat rising / flames. Why is the flame/fire used in adverts?

Environmental Studies.
– Map of an area of St. Leonards forest. Visit. Children plot things they see and decide where the dragon lived and plot that.
– What was Horsham like at the time of the sightings? Visits to Museum, Library and conduct interviews.
– What would happen if it was sighted now – people wouldn't want it – explained as something else.

Music.
Compile a tape of dragon sounds using instruments and own inventions.

DRAGONS

Maths.
area / size / shape.

Art.
Design a video cover for the film of the book "Green Smoke" by Rosemary Manning.
– Make a dragon mask.

P.E. / Drama.
Movement and role play using masks the children have made. What are their feelings? More confident with something to hide behind? Does mask change them? Are they still the same underneath?

Computer.
Front Page Extra
In groups the children write a newspaper report based on the story of St. George. Stories are written from the view of the different characters. e.g George, Dragon, Princess. Compare the reports – all make the story sound different – which is true?

Figure 9 Adapted from 'Dragons' – A Project Plan Integrating Media Education, Age Group 7–8 Year Olds', by Ann Lines, Chesworth County Junior School, Horsham, Sussex; in *Media Education in Primary Schools 2*, Occasional Papers for Teachers of English in West Sussex, Horsham Professional Centre/BFI.

By the level of fourth year juniors, you could be working towards a more conscious and explicit use of these three aspects of media. Depending on how many opportunities children have had for media work, they might be expected to have used a number of different media technologies and be able to make choices about the appropriate ones to use for different purposes. They could be familiar with visual conventions and symbols and have had some experience of constructing narratives in sounds and/or images, and of editing, if only of image sequences as in a tape-slide. They will in any case have a broader experience of the different ways in which texts can reach audiences, but you could have extended this by introducing material such as radio drama or documentary, independent video, and films shown in a cinema; as well as having given them opportunities to try to reach different audiences for their own productions. Both through talk and through their own production experience, they could have a much better idea of the different roles involved in producing a film or a television programme, and could have some understanding of media industries and be able to identify different TV companies, radio stations or film distributors, for example. The aspect that may still be quite difficult for them could be representation, although the more experience they have had in the discussion of texts and in practice and production, the more likely it is that they will see why this is a complex and contested area which they will have to go on thinking about and discussing. Their experiences of stereotyping and bias should certainly go beyond identification and rejection. They should at least be beginning to think about alternatives and counter-arguments.

▬ *Key Stage 3* ▬

Although the National Curriculum currently confines specific requirements for media work to English, I believe that sooner or later it will be impossible to resist the logic of extending media education across the curriculum. The existence of the National Curriculum and the forward planning that this will demand, actually makes such a development more likely. What is demanded in English now is so obviously limited and relates so oddly to everyone's real media experience, that pressure for change is bound to come both from within the subject area and outside it. An important factor in how media education develops in the secondary school is the existence, and growing popularity, of Media Studies courses in GCSE, BTEC and A Level, and as modules within many TVEI and CPVE schemes. For many pupils, these lead to courses in further or higher education that may have a vocational or an academic emphasis or may combine the two. The presence of specialists teaching media at Key Stage 4 often means that media work develops in the lower school, and not necessarily in English.

National Curriculum documentation so far reveals some obvious locations for media work in different subjects. My analysis of the Queen Elizabeth portrait in Chapter 2 demonstrated, I hope, that media education approaches make an important contribution to the understanding of historical evidence; as well as showing that media education ought to include an understanding of the role of media texts in the past. The brief outline of media technologies in Chapter 4 should have indicated how media production work must involve making choices about appropriate technologies, and may well involve finding all kinds of solutions to the problems of limited equipment, space and time. The physics, chemistry and electronics of media technologies draw from, and could contribute to, the science curriculum. One of the most important areas for the exploration of representation is in Geography, not only through the critical analysis of media representations of different peoples and parts of the world, but also through understanding maps and plans as texts representing aspects of the real world. Any media production work, but especially animation, requires mathematical skills and understanding in order to synchronise word and image and to achieve accurate timing. Media consumption surveys also use mathematics and statistics. Developing an understanding of media institutions and the financial background to media production ought to be an important part of economic and industrial awareness. English has never been a particularly good location for fully developing the creative and expressive aspects of the media, compared with the Art Department. Video and audio tape have often been used to record performing arts in schools – dance, drama and music – but the notion that this *mediates* the performance, turning it into a different kind of text, rather than a mere record, is rarely explored. Every subject on the curriculum now has to contend with, or take advantage of, the fact that its subject matter is represented in the media; children bring to school ideas, accurate or not, about science, history, sport and many other subjects, derived not only from documentaries but from fiction and entertainment.

The danger inherent in this mass of connections and possibilities is that media education may simply vanish into the curriculum like water into sand. The full potential of media education across the curriculum is only likely to be realised where schools can initiate a whole-school policy for media and, if possible, identify an individual as responsible for that policy and the INSET relating to it. It is likely to be further strengthened when pairs or groups of departments find ways of working together systematically on projects or themes that contain media education elements, perhaps even using these as the means of bringing their specialisms together. Combining humanities subjects at Key Stage 3 is an established scenario; but media education offers ways of linking English or other arts subjects with maths, science or technology. Where schools are looking for new ways of enabling departments to co-operate more closely and of combining attainment targets, media education could provide interesting answers.

▬ *Conclusion* ▬

Extravagant claims are made for media education. It is said that it is an intrinsically progressive subject, that must sooner or later revolutionise the way knowledge and power are taught about and understood in schools. Sometimes I have seen work in schools that justified such claims. But I also know that media education can be narrowly defined and taught unimaginatively. Like anything else, it can be taught in authoritarian and boring ways.

Media education in Key Stages 1–3 is still very new. Up to now it has appeared where there were enthusiasts who wanted to teach it – and when they moved on, it often vanished with them. There is now a legal requirement to teach what I would call a small bit of media education, within the English curriculum. By the time you read this, other bits may have been enshrined in other subjects. How these requirements get interpreted and built on is going to be up to the people doing the actual teaching and learning.

Public debate about the media in Britain is still abysmally simplistic. Agitation from the world's tackiest popular press about the world's most respected public service broadcasting system still gets taken seriously. Media monopolies and Western cultural imperialism are ignored. Vast public subsidy of high art continues while children's television stands on the brink of extinction. The idea of burning books can still invoke heartfelt moral condemnation, but the failure to nurture and protect other media is to my mind the equivalent of a literary holocaust. Media education is often seen as a way of defending children from television. It ought to be seen as a way of giving them high expectations of television, of all media, and of themselves.

Resources

Lists of teaching materials and resources for media education are available from a number of sources including the following:

Albany Video Distribution
The Albany
Douglas Way
London SE8 4AG   081 692 6322

Arts Council of Great Britain
Education Officers (Film, Video and Broadcasting; Visual Arts)
14 Great Peter Street
London SW1P 3NG   071 333 0100

Birmingham Film and Video Workshop
2nd Floor, Pitman Buildings
161 Corporation Street
Birmingham B4 6PT   021 233 3423

British Film Institute (Education Department for teaching materials and advice; Film and Video Library for cinema and TV material)
21 Stephen Street
London W1P 1PL   071 255 1444

Cinema of Women
31 Clerkenwell Close
London EC1R 0AT

English and Media Centre
Sutherland Street
London SW1V 4LH   071 828 8560

Film Education
37–39 Oxford Street
London W1R 1RE   071 434 9932

MOMI Education
Museum of the Moving Image
South Bank
London SE1 8XT   071 928 3535

Media Education Centre
5, Llandaff Road
Canton
Cardiff CF1 9NF   0222 396288

National Museum of Film, Photography and Television
(Education Department)
Princes View
Bradford BD5 0TR   0274 732277/727488

Northern Ireland Film Council
7 Lower Crescent
Belfast BT7 1NR   0232 232444

Scottish Film Council
74 Victoria Crescent Road
Dowanhill
Glasgow G12 9JN   041 334 4445

Thames Television, Central Television and the BBC have all
produced useful schools programmes on aspects of media
education; Television South and S4C have produced teaching
packs. Advice on resources may also be obtainable from your
Regional Arts Association Board.

Further Reading

David Buckingham (ed), *Watching Media Learning* (Falmer
   Press, 1990)
Máire Messenger Davies, *TV is Good for Your Kids* (Hilary
   Shipman, 1989)
Bob Hodge and David Tripp, *Children and Television* (Polity
   Press, 1986)
Len Masterman, *Teaching the Media* (Comedia, 1985)
Paul Willis (ed), *Moving Culture* (Calouste Gulbenkian
   Foundation, 1990)

Texts Quoted in Chapter Headings

John Berger and Jean Mohr, *Another Way of Telling*, (Writers
   and Readers Publishing Cooperative, 1982)
Sean Day-Lewis (ed), *One Day in the Life of Television*,
   (Grafton Books, 1989)
Doris Lessing, *The Four-Gated City* (*Children of Violence*
   Book V; Macgibbon and Kee, 1969)

Timothy Mo, *An Insular Possession* (Pan, 1987)
Carolyn Steedman, *The Tidy House: Little Girls Writing* (1982;
   Virago, 1987)
Raymond Williams, *Culture and Society* (Hogarth Press, 1987)